THE LOST TEMPLE

Written by Anna Knight • Illustrated by Roger Harris

COMPLETE THE SEARCH FOR THE LOST TEMPLE

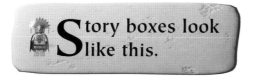

Story boxes look like this.

Puzzle boxes look like this.

Read the story and solve the puzzles on every page.
Can you solve all the puzzles and find the Lost Temple?

DK Publishing, Inc.
www.dk.com

The members of the Explorers Club clapped excitedly at the end of the slide show. "Simply fascinating! What a thrilling adventure!" they remarked as they left the Club.

Johnny Thunder and Pippin Read had just been telling about their amazing experiences traveling to all corners of the Earth as ace reporters for *World Magazine*.

"It's all very well talking about our adventures, but I want some action again," Johnny remarked to Pippin.

Just then, Doctor Kilroy rushed in. He was an old friend and adventurer from the National Museum.

"Alex Botnik from the Museum is about to contact us with details of a new expedition," he said, as he tuned the dials on the two-way radio set. Soon they heard Alex's voice, but it was a struggle to understand his message through the crackling of the radio.

THE FIRST PUZZLE

Can you figure out what the message says?

I w_s in th_ M_xic_n jungl_ s__rching for th_ r_r_ pl_nt, Curus mir_culus, wh_n I c_m_ upon som_ pr_cious r_lics of _n _nci_nt civiliz_tion. Th_r_'s _ hidd_n t_mpl_, _nd insid_, _ m_gnific_nt gold_n sun disc. Th_ t_mpl_ is not __sy to find, but I will s_nd you _ m_p _nd _rr_ng_ tr_nsport for you. B_w_r_ of S_ñor P_lom_r. H_ is working for _n _rt coll_ctor who w_nts th_ gold_n sun for hims_lf. Good luck!

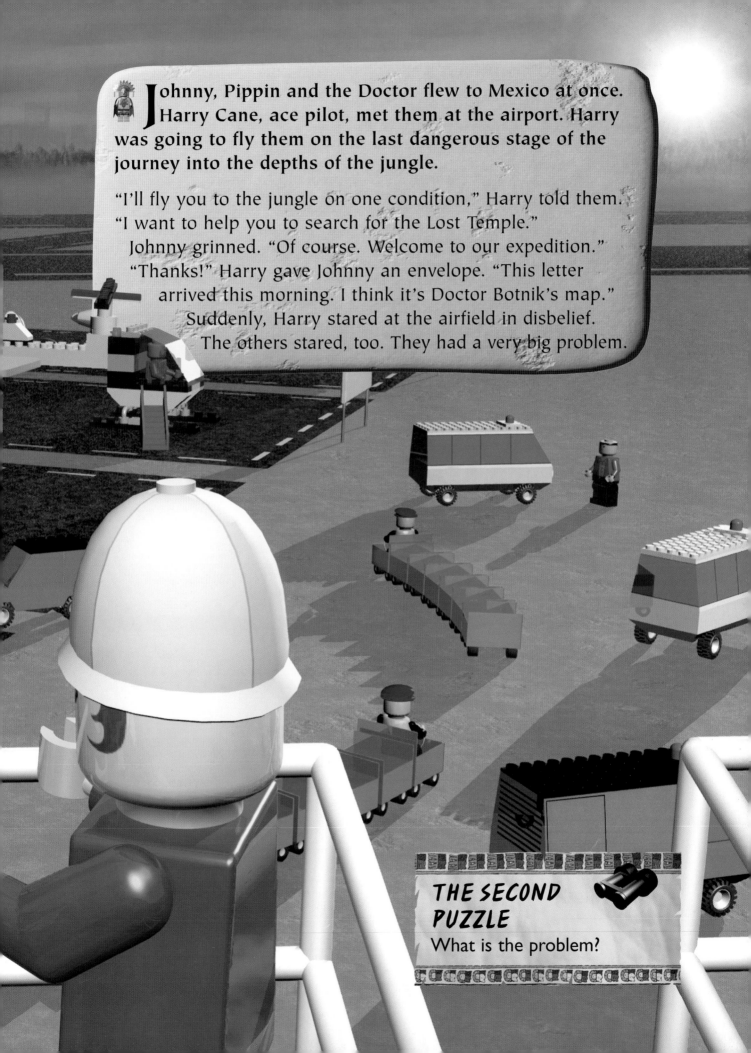

Johnny, Pippin and the Doctor flew to Mexico at once. Harry Cane, ace pilot, met them at the airport. Harry was going to fly them on the last dangerous stage of the journey into the depths of the jungle.

"I'll fly you to the jungle on one condition," Harry told them. "I want to help you to search for the Lost Temple."
Johnny grinned. "Of course. Welcome to our expedition."
"Thanks!" Harry gave Johnny an envelope. "This letter arrived this morning. I think it's Doctor Botnik's map."
Suddenly, Harry stared at the airfield in disbelief. The others stared, too. They had a very big problem.

THE SECOND PUZZLE
What is the problem?

Who had stolen Harry's plane? And why? How were they going to get to the jungle now? They had to find another plane — fast!

"Let's use that airship," said Johnny Thunder.

Doctor Kilroy made the arrangements, then they loaded the airship. Soon they were flying over the jungle. Johnny pulled out Alex Botnik's map. It was written in code.

Pippin looked over his shoulder at the map. "Look, Johnny, all we have to do to crack the code is . . ."

Pippin helped Johnny to locate the temple on the map.

The ancient ruin of Salsa Verde

Cross the bridge at Guacamole Gorge.

This is a record of my route to the Lost Temple. Sadly, I did not find the Curws miraculas, said to have the precious gift of life.

Alex

0   1km

N

THE LOST TEMPLE
Find a gift that
prickles you sore.
To give to the man
who guards the door.

Piranha Creek

Chili Waters

Deserted village

Circle of carved stone heads

THE THIRD PUZZLE
Can you decode the map?

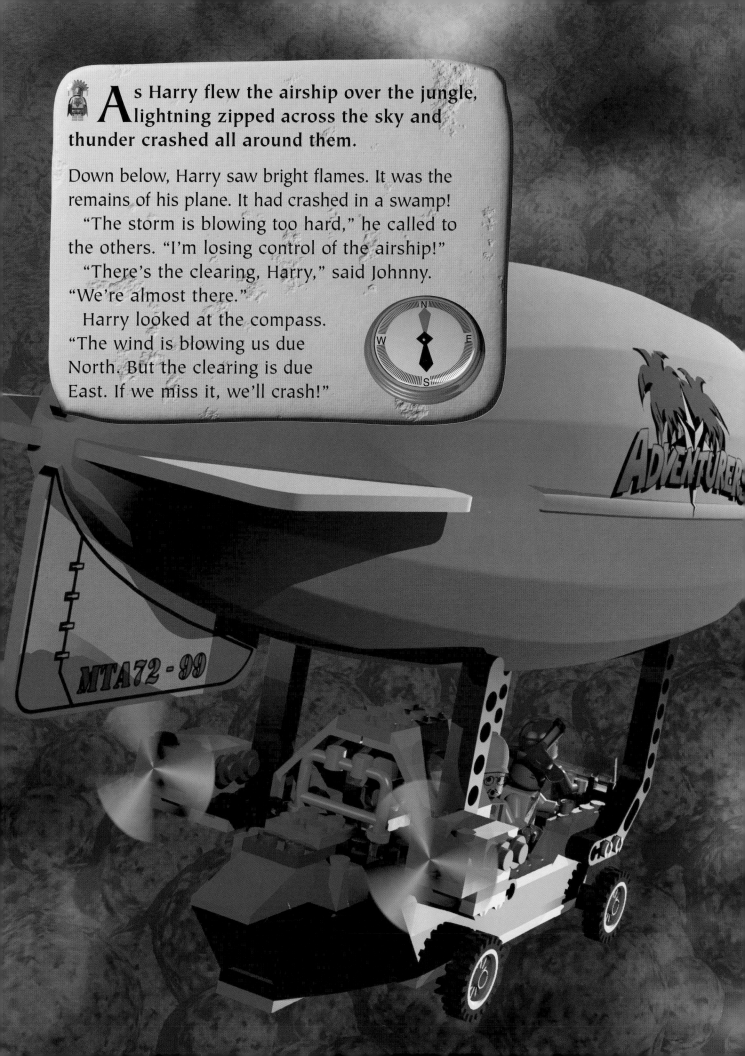

As Harry flew the airship over the jungle, lightning zipped across the sky and thunder crashed all around them.

Down below, Harry saw bright flames. It was the remains of his plane. It had crashed in a swamp!

"The storm is blowing too hard," he called to the others. "I'm losing control of the airship!"

"There's the clearing, Harry," said Johnny. "We're almost there."

Harry looked at the compass. "The wind is blowing us due North. But the clearing is due East. If we miss it, we'll crash!"

THE FOURTH PUZZLE
Should Harry turn the airship left or right in order to land safely in the clearing?

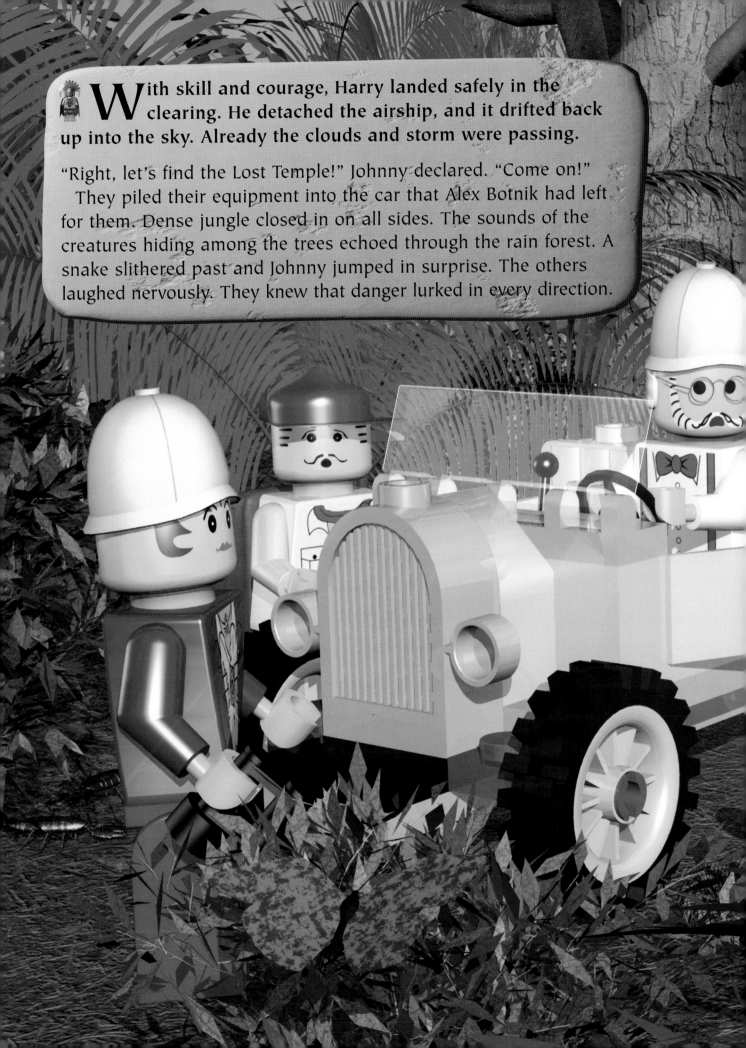

With skill and courage, Harry landed safely in the clearing. He detached the airship, and it drifted back up into the sky. Already the clouds and storm were passing.

"Right, let's find the Lost Temple!" Johnny declared. "Come on!" They piled their equipment into the car that Alex Botnik had left for them. Dense jungle closed in on all sides. The sounds of the creatures hiding among the trees echoed through the rain forest. A snake slithered past and Johnny jumped in surprise. The others laughed nervously. They knew that danger lurked in every direction.

THE FIFTH PUZZLE

How many creatures are camouflaged among the plants in the rain forest?

It was a bumpy ride over the path to Salsa Verde, the famous ancient ruin. But the track stopped at the ruin, so they'd have to find the way to the temple on foot.

"Imagine, people carved this statue thousands of years ago," said Doctor Kilroy. He gazed at the ancient ruin in awe. "Salsa Verde is such an important archaeological site."

"Someone else thinks it's important too," Johnny observed. "Someone who was here just a few minutes before us."

"I'll bet it was Señor Palomar!" Pippin exclaimed. "Alex Botnik warned us about Palomar in his message. Remember?"

THE SIXTH PUZZLE

How does Johnny know that someone else was at the Salsa Verde ruin just a few minutes earlier?

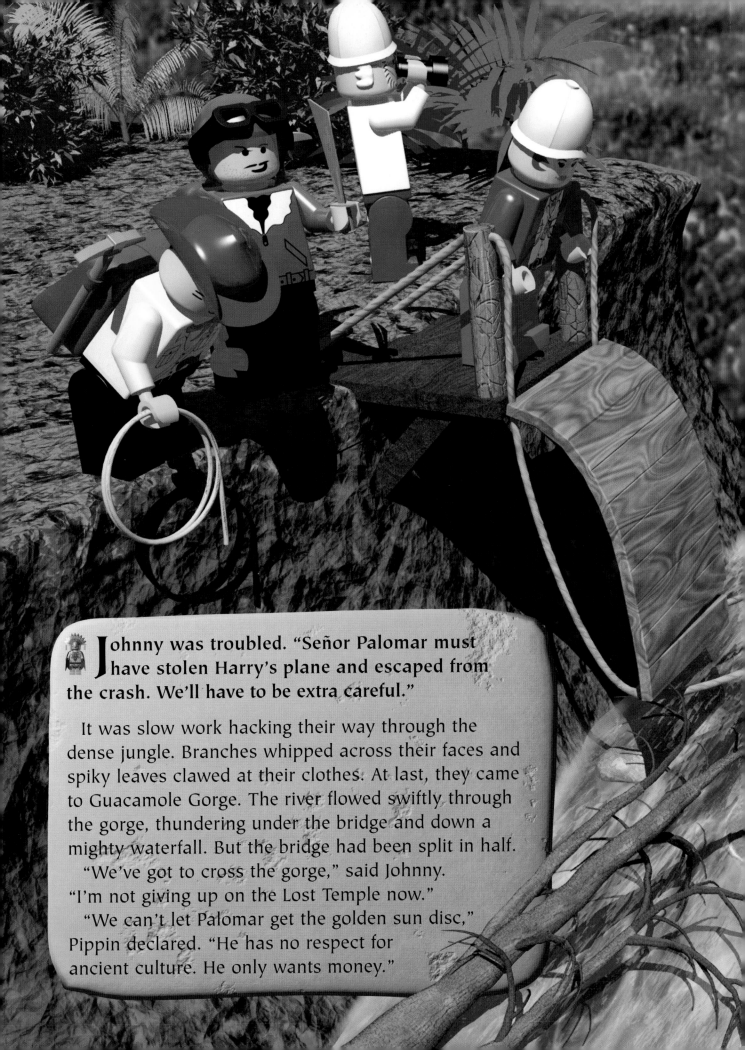

Johnny was troubled. "Señor Palomar must have stolen Harry's plane and escaped from the crash. We'll have to be extra careful."

It was slow work hacking their way through the dense jungle. Branches whipped across their faces and spiky leaves clawed at their clothes. At last, they came to Guacamole Gorge. The river flowed swiftly through the gorge, thundering under the bridge and down a mighty waterfall. But the bridge had been split in half.

"We've got to cross the gorge," said Johnny. "I'm not giving up on the Lost Temple now."

"We can't let Palomar get the golden sun disc," Pippin declared. "He has no respect for ancient culture. He only wants money."

THE SEVENTH PUZZLE

Can you figure out how to cross
Guacamole Gorge?

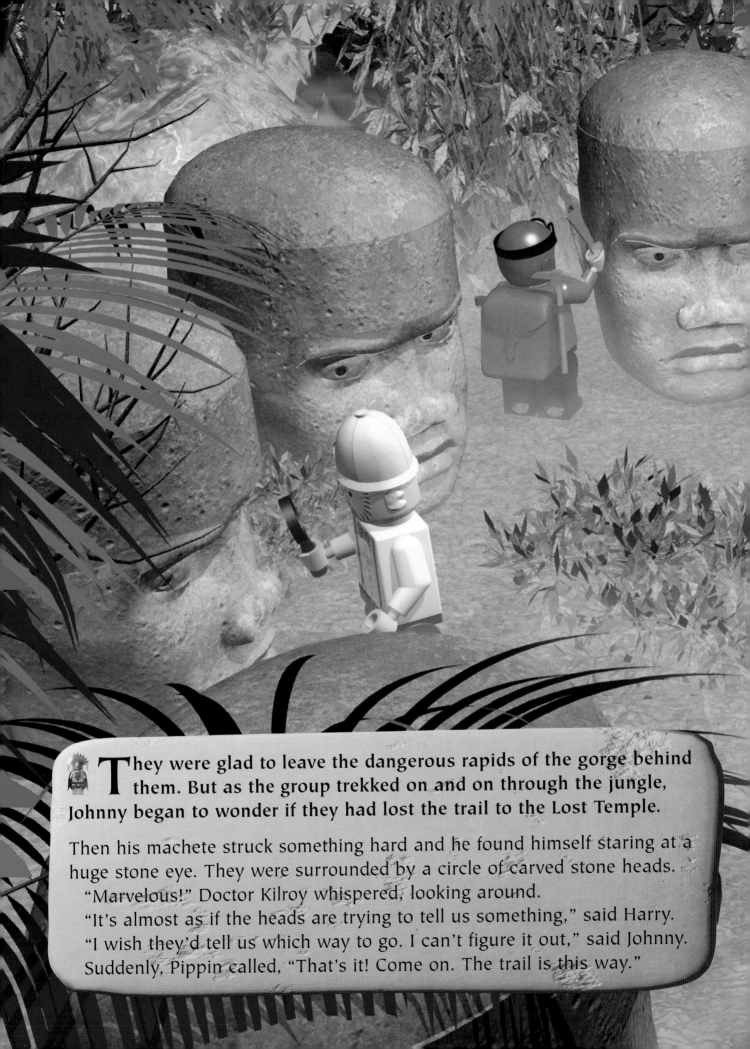

They were glad to leave the dangerous rapids of the gorge behind them. But as the group trekked on and on through the jungle, Johnny began to wonder if they had lost the trail to the Lost Temple.

Then his machete struck something hard and he found himself staring at a huge stone eye. They were surrounded by a circle of carved stone heads.

"Marvelous!" Doctor Kilroy whispered, looking around.

"It's almost as if the heads are trying to tell us something," said Harry.

"I wish they'd tell us which way to go. I can't figure it out," said Johnny.

Suddenly, Pippin called, "That's it! Come on. The trail is this way."

THE EIGHTH PUZZLE
How does Pippin know which way the trail leads?

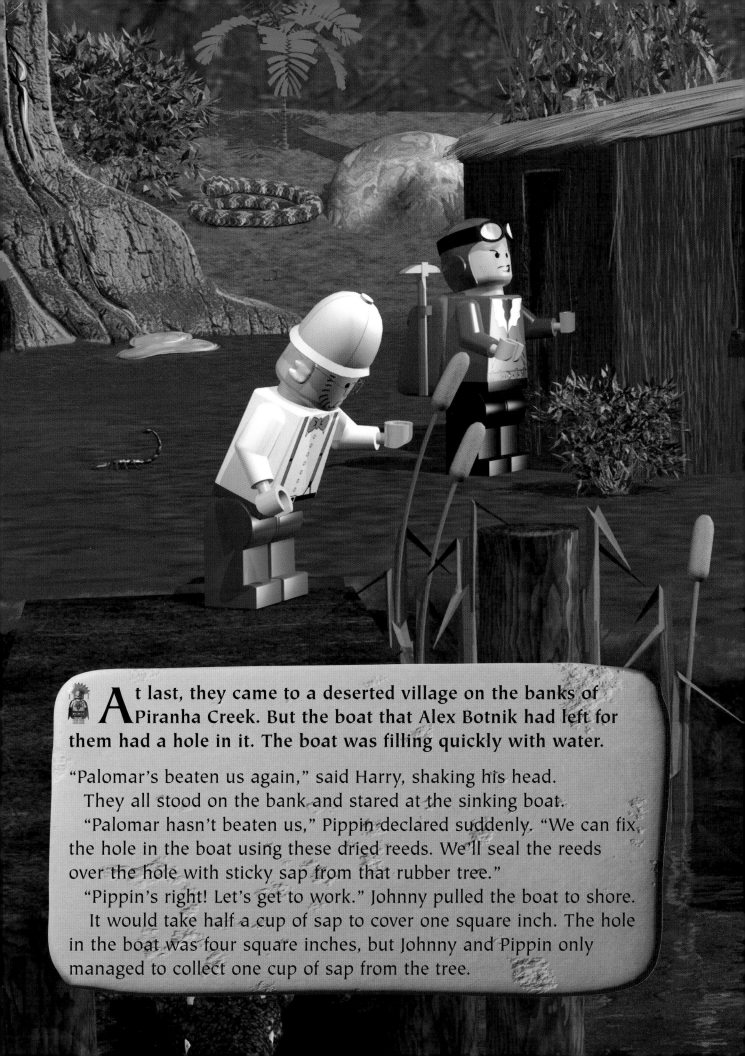

At last, they came to a deserted village on the banks of Piranha Creek. But the boat that Alex Botnik had left for them had a hole in it. The boat was filling quickly with water.

"Palomar's beaten us again," said Harry, shaking his head.
   They all stood on the bank and stared at the sinking boat.
   "Palomar hasn't beaten us," Pippin declared suddenly. "We can fix the hole in the boat using these dried reeds. We'll seal the reeds over the hole with sticky sap from that rubber tree."
   "Pippin's right! Let's get to work." Johnny pulled the boat to shore.
   It would take half a cup of sap to cover one square inch. The hole in the boat was four square inches, but Johnny and Pippin only managed to collect one cup of sap from the tree.

THE NINTH PUZZLE

How much more sticky sap would they need to completely fix the hole so the boat won't leak?

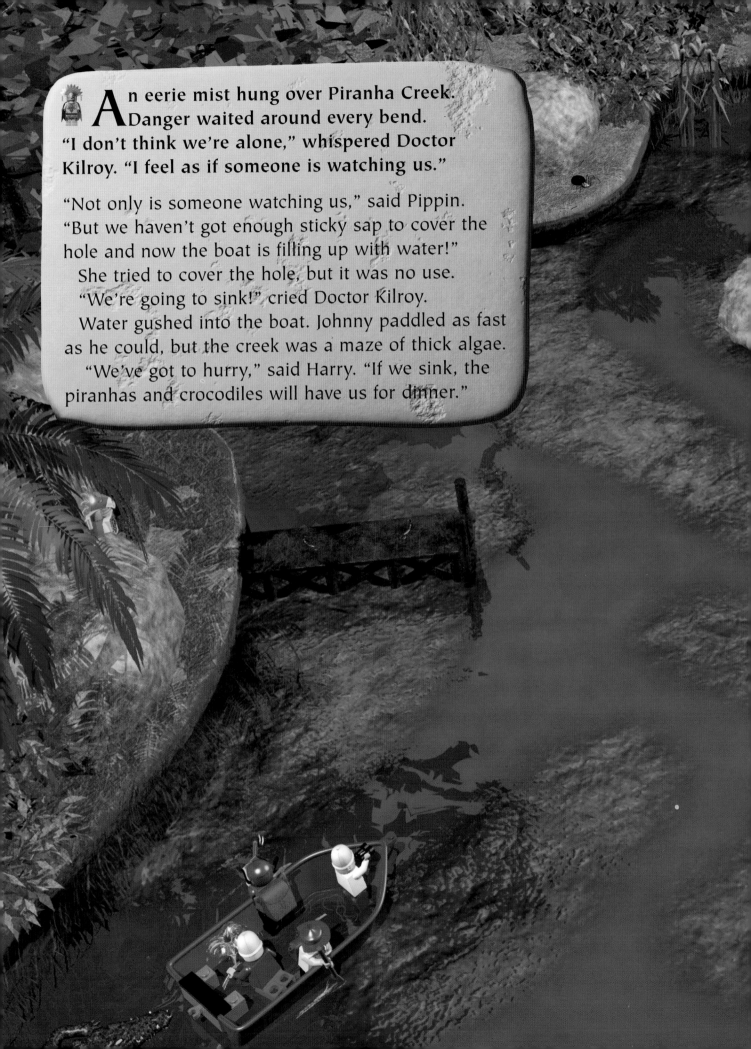

An eerie mist hung over Piranha Creek. Danger waited around every bend. "I don't think we're alone," whispered Doctor Kilroy. "I feel as if someone is watching us."

"Not only is someone watching us," said Pippin. "But we haven't got enough sticky sap to cover the hole and now the boat is filling up with water!"

She tried to cover the hole, but it was no use.

"We're going to sink!" cried Doctor Kilroy.

Water gushed into the boat. Johnny paddled as fast as he could, but the creek was a maze of thick algae.

"We've got to hurry," said Harry. "If we sink, the piranhas and crocodiles will have us for dinner."

THE TENTH PUZZLE
Find the safest and quickest route
down Piranha Creek to the stone steps.
Do you see anyone watching from the bank?

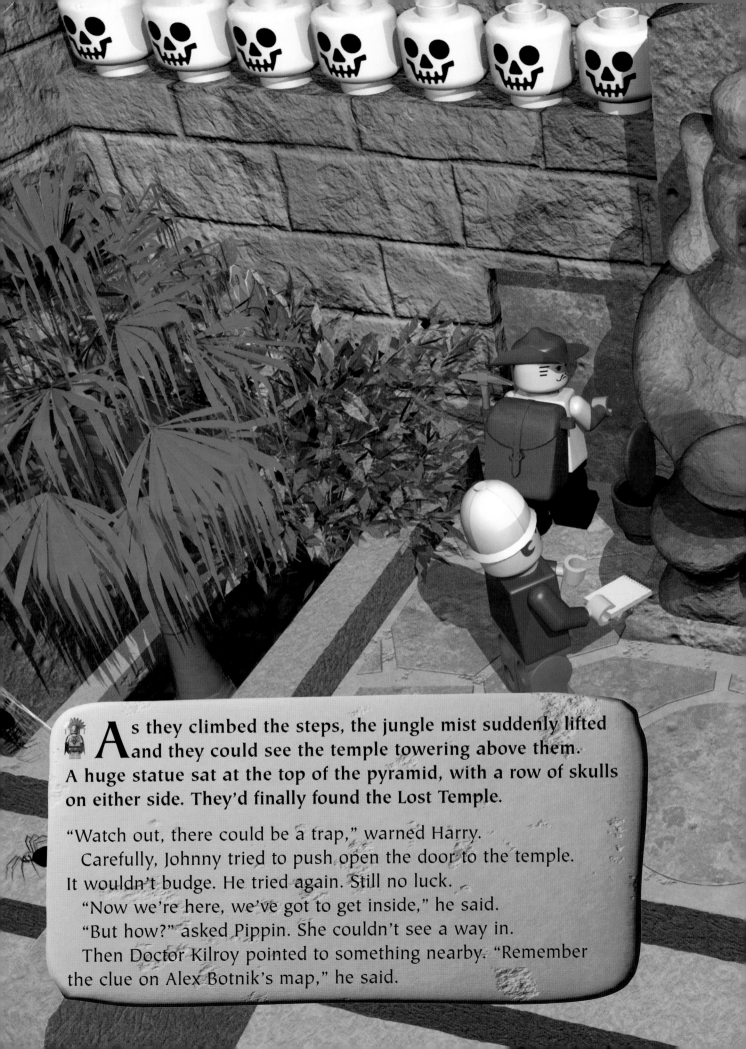

As they climbed the steps, the jungle mist suddenly lifted and they could see the temple towering above them. A huge statue sat at the top of the pyramid, with a row of skulls on either side. They'd finally found the Lost Temple.

"Watch out, there could be a trap," warned Harry.
   Carefully, Johnny tried to push open the door to the temple. It wouldn't budge. He tried again. Still no luck.
   "Now we're here, we've got to get inside," he said.
   "But how?" asked Pippin. She couldn't see a way in.
   Then Doctor Kilroy pointed to something nearby. "Remember the clue on Alex Botnik's map," he said.

THE ELEVENTH PUZZLE
How can the explorers gain entry to the Lost Temple?

A narrow panel in the temple wall slid aside. One by one, they squeezed through the gap into the temple. First Johnny, then Pippin, Doctor Kilroy, and Harry. But someone was waiting inside . . .

Within moments, Palomar and his gang had tied them all up.

"We meet at last," said Palomar. "My friends Gabarro and Villano will leave you now for the snakes to enjoy."

"Never!" shouted Pippin. She struggled defiantly.

Palomar turned to a tall stone plinth, where the sun disc blazed like fire. With an evil grin, he reached out for it.

"Stop, Palomar!" Doctor Kilroy demanded in vain.

"Don't worry," said Johnny. "He won't get away with it."

THE TWELFTH PUZZLE
Johnny has seen something that will stop Palomar. What is it?

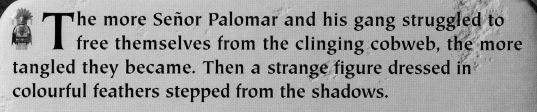**T**he more Señor Palomar and his gang struggled to free themselves from the clinging cobweb, the more tangled they became. Then a strange figure dressed in colourful feathers stepped from the shadows.

"I am Achu, Keeper of the Jungle. I protect the memory of my ancestors." As he spoke, the ropes binding Johnny and his friends untied themselves as if by magic. He raised his arm, and the sun disc blazed like fire. "Prove that you are not treasure seekers, too. Tell me, how old is this temple?"

Doctor Kilroy looked carefully at a stone tablet which showed the stages of the pyramid's construction, surrounded by bundles of reeds. "I believe each bundle symbolizes a century," he said. "In this ancient culture, a century didn't last for 100 years. It only lasted 52 years."

THE THIRTEENTH PUZZLE
Can you figure out the answer to the Keeper's question?

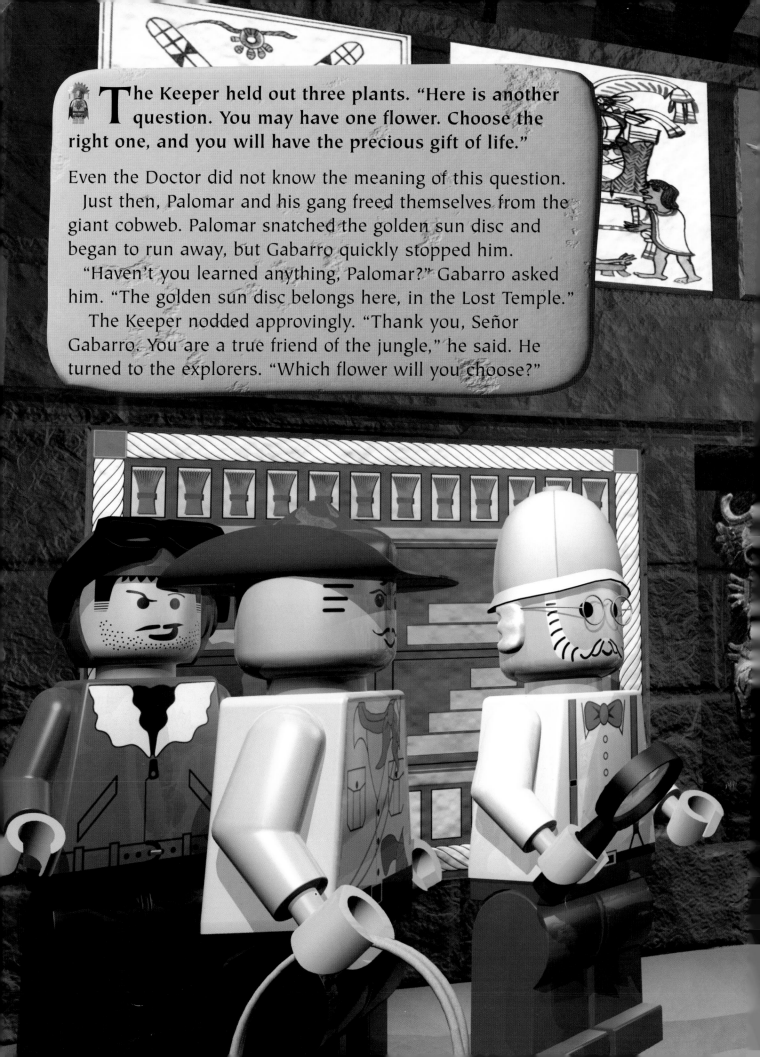

The Keeper held out three plants. "Here is another question. You may have one flower. Choose the right one, and you will have the precious gift of life."

Even the Doctor did not know the meaning of this question. Just then, Palomar and his gang freed themselves from the giant cobweb. Palomar snatched the golden sun disc and began to run away, but Gabarro quickly stopped him.

"Haven't you learned anything, Palomar?" Gabarro asked him. "The golden sun disc belongs here, in the Lost Temple."

The Keeper nodded approvingly. "Thank you, Señor Gabarro. You are a true friend of the jungle," he said. He turned to the explorers. "Which flower will you choose?"

THE FINAL PUZZLE
Which flower does Pippin choose? Why?

As their boat drifted away, Pippin clutched the *Curus miraculus* flower. Palomar and Villano ran away into the dense mist that fell over the jungle. Soon, all traces of the Lost Temple would be safely hidden once more.

CURIOUS FACTS

- The Olmecs created the first great civilization of ancient Mexico over 3000 years ago. Several huge stone heads carved by the Olmec people have been found in Mexico.

- The Aztecs called their empire *Mexica*. In 1519, Spanish conquistadors arrived, taking gold and other goods, and destroying the native people.

- The Aztecs built enormous temples in a pyramid shape. Many of these temples were hidden in dense jungle areas.

- The Aztecs did not have an alphabet – they recorded their history using pictures.

- The Aztecs played a game called *ulama*. Two teams played against each other. The ball represented the moon and the sun, while the court represented the world.

ANSWERS

THE FIRST PUZZLE

The message says: *I was in the Mexican jungle searching for the rare plant, Curus miraculus, when I came upon some precious relics of an ancient civilization. There's a hidden temple, and inside, a magnificent golden sun disc. The temple is difficult to find, but I will send a map and arrange transport for you. Beware of Señor Palomar! He is working for an art collector who wants the golden sun for himself. Good luck!*

THE SECOND PUZZLE

In the distance, someone is flying away in Harry's plane. His parking bay is empty.

THE THIRD PUZZLE

Hold the book up to a mirror to decode the map. The clues are written backward.

THE FOURTH PUZZLE

Harry must steer the airship to the right in order to reach the clearing.

THE FIFTH PUZZLE

Hiding in the jungle are: 1 monkey; 1 jaguar; 1 snake; 1 beetle; 1 ant; 2 scorpions; 2 butterflies.

THE SIXTH PUZZLE

Johnny notices the fresh apple core behind the statue, and the insects nearby preparing to eat it.

THE SEVENTH PUZZLE

The explorers can use the rope from the bridge to rappel down the left side of the bridge, landing on the stone in the middle of the river. (Or they could use Johnny's rope.) They could then use the rope on the other side of the bridge to climb up out of the gorge.

THE EIGHTH PUZZLE

The clue is in the eyes of the carved heads, which are looking toward the gap at the bottom of the page.

THE NINTH PUZZLE

They need one more cup of sap for a total of two cups, the amount needed to cover the hole.

THE TENTH PUZZLE

The line marked in white shows the safe route through Piranha Creek. Look to the left of the creek, where someone is watching from the jungle.

THE ELEVENTH PUZZLE

The clue is on the map. Place the prickly pear cactus on the statue which guards the door.

THE TWELFTH PUZZLE

Johnny sees a giant web and the picture showing the web covering the disc and trapping the villain.

THE THIRTEENTH PUZZLE

Each bundle represents 52 years and there are 14 bundles, which means the temple is 728 years old.

FINAL PUZZLE

Pippin recalls a clue on the map which leads her to choose the white flower. There is also a clue in the pictures on the wall of the temple.

A DK Publishing Book
www.dk.com
www.lego.com
First American edition, 1999
2 4 6 8 10 9 7 5 3 1
Published in the United States by DK Publishing, Inc.
95 Madison Avenue, New York, New York 10016

Designers: Nick Avery and John Kelly
Editor: Caryn Jenner
Managing Art Editor: Cathy Tincknell
Managing Editor: Joanna Devereux

ISBN 0-7894-4706-1

A catalog record is available from the Library of Congress.
Color reproduction by Dot Gradations
Printed and bound in Italy by L.E.G.O.